DORSET

Ninebarrow's

DORSET

Musical walks in a magical landscape

James LaBouchardiere & Jon Whitley

www.ninebarrowwalking.co.uk

We are also
excited to announce...

Ninebarrow

MUSICAL
WALKING
HOLIDAYS

Join us on a luxury break in the Isle of Purbeck. Enjoy stunning walks guided by *Ninebarrow*, indulge in Dorset's finest food and drink, and immerse yourself in music from a hand-picked selection of the UK's brightest folk stars.

Come and explore the magic of Purbeck...with us!

First Published 2019
© Ninebarrow 2019

Published by Yonder Stile Ltd

ISBN 978-1-9160080-0-7

A CIP catalogue record for this book is available in the British Library.

The contents of this book are believed correct at the time of printing.
Nevertheless, the publishers cannot be held responsible for any errors or
omissions or for changes in the details given in this book or for the consequences
of any reliance on the information it provides. We have tried to ensure accuracy,
but things do change occasionally - both in the landscape and with regard to
access.

If you do spot any inaccuracies, please let us know by e-mailing:

info@ninebarrow.co.uk

DISCLAIMER

We have taken all reasonable steps to ensure that the walks contained within this
book are safe and achievable by walkers with a reasonable level of fitness.
However, all outdoor activities involve a degree of risk and the publishers accept
no responsibility for any injuries caused to readers whilst following these walks.

The distances described throughout this book are for guidance only - actual
distances may exceed or be less than those described. For more advice about
walking safely and how to use this book in general, please see page 13.

The view towards Kimmeridge
as seen from Gad Cliff, near Tyneham
Walk 8

Contents

A35

A37

A35

DORCHESTER

7

● Abbotsbury

6

A354

9 ● Osmington

Chesil Beach

WEYMOUTH

POOLE

A35

WAREHAM

2 Poole Harbour

Arne

Isle of Purbeck

4

Studland

Corfe Castle

1 Old Harry Rocks

8 Tyneham

10

SWANAGE

Kimmeridge

5 Worth Matravers

3

Welcome!

Worbarrow Bay
as seen from Gold Down
Walk 8

Long before Jay and I began singing together as 'Ninebarrow', Dorset had already woven its spell around us. We were both born and bred in the county and it has played a central role in our lives for as long as we can remember. Jay was brought up living on East Blagdon Farm near Cranborne and I was brought up in Canford Heath near Poole - so both of our early childhoods were set against the backdrop of the Dorset landscape in one way or another. For Jay, the ancient woodlands and chalk escarpments of Cranborne Chase were all around him until the age of ten. For me, whilst the heath and woodland that backed on to my childhood home certainly became a key part of my growing up, it was probably more the numerous weekend family walks on which I was taken that have inspired my life-long love of the county.

Before Jay and I began making music together, one of the main things that we loved to do with our spare time was to walk. There's something about the pace of walking: gentle, rhythmic plodding through the countryside. It's just fast enough to let you explore the wonderful variety of any given landscape, but slow enough to be able to savour every moment and really absorb the myriad vistas it has to offer. We've walked all over the UK, from the charming downs of Sussex to the weathered majesty of the Isle of Skye. We'd even go as far to call the fells of the Lake District our 'home-away-from-home'. But despite this, we always look forward to returning home to Dorset: its Jurassic coastline and rolling ridges, its deep, green woodlands and its heather-strewn heathlands. It just never gets boring for us.

So when we started singing together, we decided we needed a name. 'LaBouchardiere and Whitley' just didn't quite have the snappy ring we were after!

It's funny though - at this point, we were only singing covers of other people's music and hadn't written a single song together. When Jay suggested the name 'Ninebarrow' (taken from the hill 'Nine Barrow Down', just next to Corfe Castle) we both knew straight away that it was the right choice. As I look back on it, it seems to me like that was a watershed moment: our music was now intrinsically linked with the landscape. From that day onwards, the covers we had been singing started to give way to self-penned songs inspired by Dorset - its countryside, its historical monuments and ancient burial sites, its flora and fauna.

Many of our songs have been written immediately following days out in the Dorset landscape and we decided back in 2017 that we'd love to be able to share these walks with the people who listen to our music. We wanted them to be able to visit the hawthorn tree which held the seven crows that inspired 'Blood on the Hillside'; we wanted them to be able to search the central pillar of St Aldhelm's Chapel and find the hairpins we sing about in 'The Pinner'.

And so here we are! It's a real pleasure to be able to share a little bit of Dorset's magic with you here in this book and we really hope that you get as much enjoyment from these walks as we have over the years.

See you out on the hills!

Corfe Castle at Sunset
Walk 4

See you out on the hills!

Taken any good selfies?! Why not share them with us at: info@ninebarrow.co.uk

Jay & Jon

Using This Book

TITLE

This includes the number of the walk as listed in the contents page, as well as the highlights of the route

SUMMARY

Brief notes on the duration and difficulty of the walk, as well as where to find the nearest loos and - of course - pubs to round off your excursion! **NB:** the postcodes provided may not take you to the exact location of the parking

MAP

We've included a basic map to help you reference your progress along the route. These include a selection of the other major footpaths in order to highlight potential junctions you may come across. Please note that these maps are not always to scale. We would always recommend taking a proper OS map with you (see overleaf)

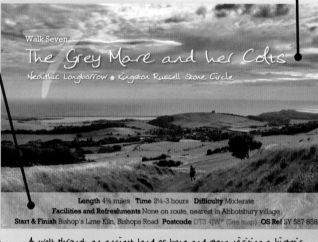

Walk Seven

The Grey Mare and her Colts

Neolithic Longbarrow ● Kingston Russell Stone Circle

Length 4½ miles **Time** 2½-3 hours **Difficulty** Moderate
Facilities and Refreshments None on route, nearest in Abbotsbury village
Start & Finish Bishop's Lime Kiln, Bishops Road **Postcode** DT3 4JW (See map) **OS Ref** SY 587 858

A walk through an ancient land of bone and stone, visiting a historic long barrow and a mysterious, Bronze Age stone circle - with magnificent views along the West Dorset Heritage Coast

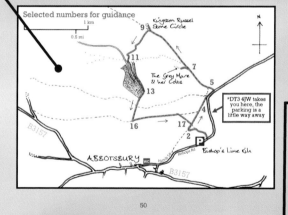

Selected numbers for guidance

1 km
0.5 mi

Kingston Russell Stone Circle
9

11

7

The Grey Mare & her Colts

13

5

*DT3 4JW takes you here, the parking is a little way away

4

16

17

2

ABBOTSBURY

Bishop's Lime Kiln

B3157

B3157

50

DIRECTIONS

We've tried to make our directions as easy to follow as possible. We've broken the route up into sections and referenced key points on the map so that you can keep track of where you are.

We want this book to feel more like a guided tour of our favourite stomping grounds, rather than simply a book of walks. We hope that, even if you've walked these trails as often as we have, you may learn something new or appreciate a feature that you'd never noticed before!

♪ To the Stones

We have a fantastic organisation called 'Dorset Artsreach' in our neck of the woods which brings the arts to many rural locations around the county. They were part of a project called 'The Land of Bone and Stone', designed to raise awareness of the rich archaeological heritage of the South Dorset Ridgeway - a 17-mile stretch of chalk downland. We were commissioned to write a series of songs that would help to raise public awareness of this amazing ceremonial landscape.

'To the Stones' was inspired by a Neolithic long barrow called 'The Grey Mare and Her Colts' on the Ridgeway just above Abbotsbury. It tells of a family taking their child up to this important monument for the first time. Not simply a house for the dead, it's introduced to the child as an integral part of the community, where they will be able to find spiritual strength and support throughout their lives.

SONG NOTES

One of the main reasons we wanted to write this book was to share with others how the landscape we love has inspired the music we make. If you haven't already got our albums, then you'll be able to find them at the shop on our website!

The parking spot for this walk is a place called 'Bishop's Lime Kiln'. You reach it by following the minor road, north-east out of Abbotsbury for about a mile. The car park is on the left. At the back of it is...well...a lime kiln! We haven't really been able to find out anything else about it, but it was presumably once used to make quicklime for agricultural use.

1. Walk out on to the road, turning left up the hill for 10 yards or so, before turning immediately left onto a track that leads to a metal gate and wooden signpost. Climb the stile adjacent to the gate and head west for approximately 300 yards, keeping the slope of the field's higher tier directly to your right.

THE VIEW. To the south-east is the bulky western side of the Isle of Portland, south-west is Abbotsbury and St Catherine's Chapel; directly south is Chesil Beach (all of which are discussed in greater detail in Walk 6).

INFO: MEDIEVAL LYNCHETS

Medieval Lynchets — The fields here are largely tiered due to their historic agricultural use. These wide strip farming 'lynchets' probably date to the Medieval period. There is some debate as to whether they were dug or formed naturally as sections of the hillside were ploughed repeatedly - but either way - they make for an interesting hillside!

51

QR CODES

There are some features in the landscape which deserve more column inches than we can spare in the book. If you have a QR reader on your phone, scan the codes and you'll be taken to a web page where space is less of a premium!

INFO BOXES

While it's important to know where you're going on a route, it's also nice to know what you're looking at! Our handwritten side notes aren't essential info, but hopefully help to pick out some extra highlights on the route.

Staying Safe

All the walks in this book are suitable for any reasonably fit person and the routes themselves are pretty easy to follow. That said, we really do advise that you take an Ordnance Survey (OS) map with you, in addition to this book. Our maps are hand-drawn, and are for reference only.

The OS Map that covers all of these walks is:

OS Explorer OL 15 'Purbeck and South Dorset'

Obviously, no walking activity can be truly free from risk and a wee bit of common sense is needed when heading out for a walk in the countryside! Here are a few things we always do and always take when we're heading out onto the hills:

- **Check the weather forecast**
And be prepared for the odd shower, even if the forecast says it should be dry - Purbeck seems to have its own microclimate and we get caught out every now and again!

- **Sensible footwear**
We don't consider these walks to be too challenging, but we'd still advise wearing walking boots, or at least sturdy walking shoes.

- **A good waterproof jacket**
Just in case you get caught out!

- **A torch**
Just in case it takes you longer than expected to get back

- **A compass**
We try not to reference compass points too much in our descriptions, however, sometimes it's the only way to make sure you're heading in the right direction!

- **First aid kit**

- **Some nibbles & plenty of water**

- **Fully charged mobile phone**
But don't rely on it for your compass or maps - phones have a tendency to run out of battery just when you need them.

- **Don't forget your camera**
There are some amazing views on these walks!

Please bear in mind that many of these walks will take you through working farmland which may contain livestock. Give these animals a wide berth

Lastly: a number of walks in this book use cliff paths.
Don't be tempted to stray off them to get a better view.
Some of the cliffs overhang, and it's difficult to tell if what you're standing on is safe!

Walk One

Studland

Old Harry Rocks • Fort Henry • Ballard Down

Length 5 miles **Time** 2-2½ hours **Difficulty** Easy (with one moderate climb)
Toilets See Map **Refreshments** The Bankes Arms; The Pig on the Beach
Start & Finish National Trust South Beach Car Park **Postcode** BH19 3AU **OS Ref** SZ 037 825

One of our very favourite walks. We usually prefer to climb up out of
Studland first, then enjoy an easy downhill walk all the way back to
the pub at the end.

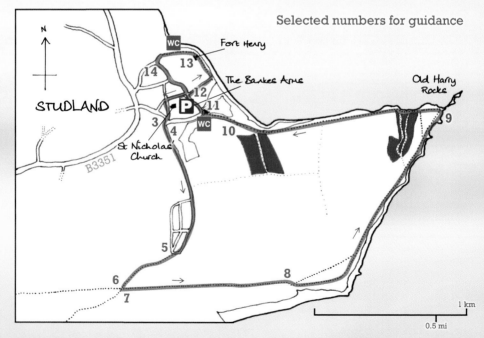

Selected numbers for guidance

♪ Blood on the Hillside

'Blood on the Hillside' is a song that came straight out of the Purbeck Hills. We were out walking on a bleak, autumn day when we came across a particularly windswept hawthorn - in which we saw a veritable 'murder' of crows; seven to be exact.

We had the old nursery rhyme 'One For Sorrow' bouncing around our heads and we got to thinking about what that 'secret never to be told' might actually be.

Murder seemed like the natural thing on a day like that! As we slowly made our way to the pub, the story of the song came together: a body found by local villagers lies below a tree holding seven crows. As the sun rises above the hillside, rumours spread of witches in the night and, with seven women of the village missing, the crows - still unmoving in the branches - are quickly viewed with suspicion.

Shape-changing witches? Well the villagers think so...

There are quite a few car parks in and around Studland, but by far the easiest place to park is the large National Trust car park next to The Bankes Arms.

Stone Cross
Studland

1. At the far right hand corner of the car park (with your back to the road) you'll find a gate. Go through this and towards the grave yard of St Nicholas' Church. If you've got time - do pop in to have a look at the church. It's absolutely beautiful and has hosted a few Ninebarrow concerts over the years!

2. Head through the churchyard, underneath the yew trees and, after a few minutes, the path will go steeply downhill emerging onto School Lane, where you should turn left down the hill.

3. After a few hundred yards you'll reach a large stone cross. It's a modern monument, although it is supposedly built on the foundations of an ancient Saxon one.

4. With this on your left, dogleg right, and then left, past Manor Farm and take the road leading up the hill. Continue upwards with hedgerows on your left, passing the Glebeland Estate on your right. It's a steep start to the walk, but the views will be worth it, we promise!

5. The path bends slightly to the right and at the top you'll see a gate. Go through, taking the main rocky path which begins to lead you up the northern flank of Ballard Down.

THE VIEW: If you need a breather, have a rest halfway up and glance over your shoulder, where you'll be rewarded with beautiful views out over Studland Bay and Poole Harbour. The largest of the Islands you'll be able to see is Brownsea Island and, if you bring your gaze directly downwards from it, you'll be able to spot Little Sea: an enclosed freshwater lake, cut off from the sea by the ever-growing dunes of Studland beach.

6. Continue up the hill and follow the track as the grassy hillside begins to open up around you. Aim for the signpost at the brow of the hill.

THE VIEW: The views here are not quite as panoramic because the looming bulk of Ballard Down behind blocks the view to the west. But it's pretty impressive, nonetheless! Swanage Bay greets you to the south, while Godlingston Heath unfolds to the north, giving way to Poole Harbour. To the east, if the visibility is being kind, you will see the Isle of Wight ahead.

7. Head east, descending gently across the top of the hillside, following signs to 'Old Harry'.

INFO: BLOOD ON THE HILLSIDE
You'll pass two way-marker stones on your left, the second of which bears the weathered inscription 'Studland Manor 1776'. It is just after this stone marker that the hawthorn tree responsible for inspiring our song 'Blood on the Hillside' can be found. There are two in quite quick succession, but it is the latter and more windswept of the two that held the seven crows on the cold November day we saw them. As we've said many times on stage, we had actually almost finished writing the song by the time we reached the end of this walk! With a thick mist hanging over Rempstone Heath to the northwest, we used other elements of the landscape to inspire the verses as we walked.

8. Follow the path through a gate with two round barrows and a series of broken stones on the right. Continue until you reach a triangulation pillar.

STUDLAND BAY AND WW2

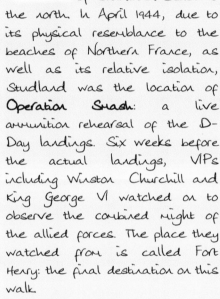

Operation Smash

As the path continues eastward, you've got a bit of time to absorb the huge size of Studland Beach to the north. In April 1944, due to its physical resemblance to the beaches of Northern France, as well as its relative isolation, Studland was the location of **Operation Smash**: a live ammunition rehearsal of the D-Day landings. Six weeks before the actual landings, VIPs including Winston Churchill and King George VI watched on to observe the combined might of the allied forces. The place they watched from is called Fort Henry: the final destination on this walk.

9. When the path reaches the triangulation pillar, it splits. You can go through the gate on the right to join the Coast Path as it curves around the clifftop, but for the best views, we prefer to fork left and down the middle of the broad grassy hillside. Both routes lead to 'Old Harry'.

INFO: OLD HARRY ROCKS

Old Harry Rocks

There are various theories relating to how this name came about. One legend suggested that the Devil (sometimes called Old Harry) slept on the rocks. Another links the rocks with the infamous Poole Pirate, Harry Paye. We rather like the former - it certainly seems to fit the tone of 'Blood on the Hillside'!

10. After you've explored the headland, turn your back on Old Harry and follow the main path westward. Ignore any minor paths leading out to the cliff edge. Follow the main path for about a mile.

Inside Fort Henry

11. After a mile or so along the flat track, the grassy path eventually gives way to broken tarmac and begins to descend. Follow the path until you reach the public toilets in Studland Village, on your right

12. Turn right up the hill, passing The Bankes Arms on your left (you may want to return here later!).

13. Opposite the car park, just after Holme Dean House, there is a clear path on the right that leads to Fort Henry.

INFO: FORT HENRY

Fort Henry is really more of a bunker and, when you first find it nestled down on the end of Redend Point, it seems completely out of place! It was given its rather grand title by the Royal Canadian Engineers who built it in 1943 and named it after their home base in Ontario. This observation bunker is the spot from which Churchill and the other VIPS watched Operation Smash, though its main purpose was to protect the bay from possible German invasion.

Fort Henry

14. After exploring, you can retrace your steps to the car park but if you'd like to carry on a little further, continue along the path to the west and to the NT's Middle Beach car park.

15. On your left you'll find 'The Groom's House', which the NT has recently opened as a second-hand book shop, as well as giving you the opportunity to see the meagre lodgings of Studland Manor's groom. After this, turn left and stay on Manor Road. You'll pass the old Manor House on the left (now the swanky 'Pig on the Beach' restaurant) before reaching the NT car park next to The Bankes Arms. Time for a pint? Of course it is! ●

The view from Ballard Down
towards Studland Bay

OLD HARRY 1¾

STUDLAND 1

SZ03 4813

Arne
RSPB Nature Reserve ● Poole Harbour

Length 4 miles   **Time** 1½-2 hours   **Difficulty** Easy
Toilets RSPB Arne Car Park   **Refreshments** RSPB Café and Visitor Centre
Start & Finish RSPB Arne Car Park   **Postcode** BH20 5BJ   **OS Ref** SY 972 878

This easy amble through a stunning RSPB nature reserve on the western fringes of Poole Harbour is proof that you don't need to climb hundreds of feet for stunning views. With rare birds like the Dartford Warbler in residence, it's definitely worth bringing your binoculars!

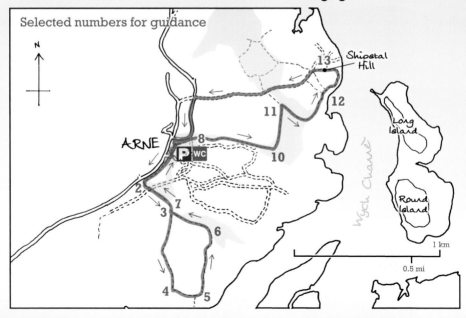

♪ Birdsong

When we first started performing as Ninebarrow, we were given an old set of choral manuscripts that used to be owned by Jay's Granny. One of the collections was called 'Bird Songs' and within it was a song called 'Wood Pigeon'. We thought the lyrics, attributed to someone known only as 'A.S.', were really beautiful in their simplicity and we used them as the basis for this song. It captures perfectly the feeling of some of our favourite woodland walks in Dorset.

The easiest way to park for this walk is to pony up and pay the £5 charge in the RSPB car park. If you're a member you get free parking. The alternative is leaving your car somewhere along the main Arne Road. You're not allowed to park in the passing places, but there are a few spots on the run down to the car park that are suitable. It'll just add another quarter mile to the beginning and end of the walk.

This walk is split into two distinct halves: the first taking in the heathland to the south of the Arne peninsula, and the second enjoying the wooded areas to the north-east.

1. Assuming you're starting from the car park, head south-west out of it, following the sign to Combe Heath. Pass through a gate, and into the field that doubles as an overflow car park.

Towards Round Island
from the Arne Peninsula

2. Head through the wooden gate at the far end, towards the pine trees behind it. Take the path left, continuing to follow the signs for Combe Heath. Follow the sandy track which will gradually curve to the right, ignoring any paths on the left.

3. At the split, take the right fork slightly uphill until you reach a bench with a view out over the harbour.

THE VIEW: Directly ahead in the far distance, you'll be able to spot Corfe Castle, almost camouflaged, nestling snuggly with West Hill to its right and East Hill to its left; the latter continues upwards to become Nine Barrow Down. If you've done any of the other walks in this book that involve climbing those hills, this vantage point makes their height seem quite understated, though it certainly doesn't feel that way when you're walking on (and up!) them. The bench also provides a good vantage point down to one of the many arms of Poole Harbour, Middlebere Lake. It looks like an estuary at first, but the four rivers (Frome, Piddle, Corfe and Sherford) that drain into the Harbour do so elsewhere.

4. After enjoying the view, continue along the track, until you reach a sign for 'Viewing Screen'.

5. Here, turn left past the bench and begin to head north, with the Purbeck ridge to your back.

6. The path will descend gently downward with trees to either side, before curving to the left to complete the loop around Combe Heath.

7. When you meet the path on which you began the heathland loop, follow it all the way back to the main car park. Walk through the car park to the far end, passing the visitor centre on your left. Follow signs for 'Shipstal Trails'.

8. Turn right up the hill and into the woodland keeping to the right and ignoring the tarmac track on the left. At the top of the rise there is a gap in the trees to your right with another beautiful view out to the Purbeck ridge, Corfe Castle now far to the right.

9. Follow the path as it meanders generally eastward. You'll begin to follow a fence on the left, with a field beyond it, while the views of the Purbeck Hills will gradually be obscured by gorse and trees. Keep to the main path and don't be tempted to turn off to the left or right.

10. The track will turn almost 90 degrees to the left. Continue to keep the field and fence on your left until you reach a red and green marker post.

11. Here there is a confluence of tracks. Look to your right and you'll spot another red and green marker post; take the path towards it but keep the post on your left as you begin to head east. The path will eventually curve to the left, and you'll pass two benches on the right.

THE VIEW: Here you'll get excellent views of two of the harbour's islands: 'Long' on the left and 'Green' on the right, both of which are privately owned.

12. Follow the path past a third bench and past another red and green post. Here there is access to the beach. After exploring, continue following the red and green posts as the path meanders above the shoreline, before eventually turning inland, taking you up to the stone plinth of the viewpoint on Shipstal Hill.

THE VIEW: This is a really lovely vantage point to take in views of the harbour and Brownsea Island now visible to the east, with Hamworthy and Poole's ferry terminal to the north-east.

13. From the back of the viewpoint, take the track marked with the red and green posts down the steps to rejoin the main path. The route back to the car park is now clearly signposted to the left and is just under a mile. Further signs to the car park will guide you back. ●

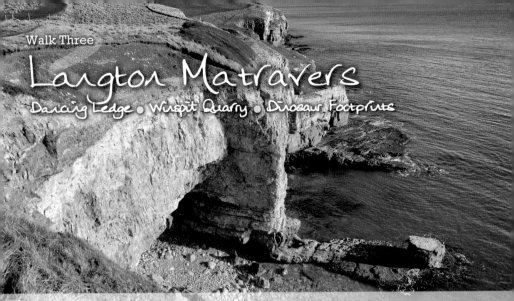

Walk Three
Langton Matravers
Dancing Ledge • Wuspit Quarry • Dinosaur Footprints

Length 4½ miles **Time** 2-3 hours **Difficulty** Moderate
Toilets Worth Matravers Car Park **Refreshments** Square & Compass, Worth Matravers
Start & Finish National Trust Spyway Car Park **Postcode** BH19 3HG **OS Ref** SY 997 783

A loop which takes in the famous Dancing Ledge, views of the old stone quarry of Wuspit, and the ancient ridge path of the Priest's Way - and even some dinosaur footprints!

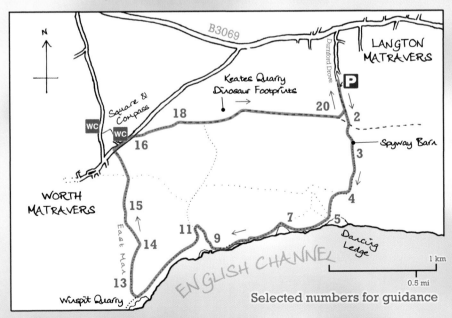

♪ Halsewell

On the 6th January 1786, an East Indiaman called the Halsewell ran aground off the coast of Dorset, near Winspit. Faced with an unprecedented blizzard, the sailors should have gone aloft to furl the sails of the three-masted ship so that it could be brought under control. This didn't happen.

In 'The Unfortunate Captain Peirce', which details the entire sorry tale, author Phillip Browne discusses the possibility that discontent within the crew led to this fateful mistake. The sailors were left with no option but to cut down two of the masts, and subsequently, with a damaged rudder and their third mast lost to the storm, the ship sank.

Amazingly, a small number of hardy sailors scaled the sheer cliff face, alerting local quarrymen, who came out in the middle of the raging storm and managed to lift 88 men from the water. However, Captain Peirce and his daughters were among the 168 who drowned or were dashed on the rocks. It is still Dorset's worst shipping disaster.

To find the car park, head east through Langton Matravers on the B3069. Turn right on to Durnford Drove. Follow the road until it becomes a narrower track. Follow this all the way up to the Spyway Car Park

1. From the Spyway National Trust car park, head south-east up the main track, towards the Spyway Farm Estate.

2. When you reach a junction in the path, and the 4-way sign post, head straight on, following the sign to 'Dancing Ledge'. Dogleg left and then right up towards Spyway Barn, passing the house on your left.

INFO: SPYWAY BARN

The barn was used by smugglers to store contraband brought up from the coast, before being moved inland to Langton Matravers, where, legend has it, it was then stored in the church roof! (See below)

St. George's Church
Langton Matravers

3. Pass through the gate and into the field beyond the barn, with the sea visible in the distance. Continue through a gap in the drystone wall and into a second field, where the view of the sea begins to expand as you head downhill.

4. Pass through the kissing gate at the end of the field and follow the rocky path downhill to the right as it winds down towards the sea.

5. Going down to Dancing Ledge requires clambering over a stile, and a bit of a scramble down. It's worth it though!

INFO: DANCING LEDGE

The ledge supposedly gets its name from the fact that when waves wash over the rocky shelf, the furrows in the surface of the rock cause the water to bob about, making the ledge appear to dance. It was previously a Purbeck Stone quarry. More information about the local quarries can be found on Walk 5, page 41. It's not really safe to swim in the sea here because of the strong currents, but a rectangular area was blasted out with dynamite by one of the local preparatory schools in 1906 and was allegedly used for early morning swimming before chapel.

Dancing Ledge

6. Climb back up and re-join the coast path, heading west.

THE VIEW: As the path continues westward, the larger quarry at Winspit becomes visible in the distance, with the bulk of St Aldhelm's Head beyond. Medieval strip farming 'lynchets' score the side of East Man in the distance (find out more about these in Walk 7, on page 51).

7. Continue towards Seacombe and as you reach the next gate, you'll pass another small quarry on the left. If you look down, you'll spot a ship's cannon lying next to the cliff edge below. Presumably this is from one of the many ships that have foundered on this coastline, although we've not managed to discover which one.

8. Continue along the coast path and through two more gates, until you see the rock shelf and caves of Seacombe Quarry directly in front of you.

9. Bear right here and continue inland for a hundred yards or so passing a stone waymarker and a gate on the left.

DETOUR

The gate leads into the quarry, which you may wish to explore if you've got the time.

The view from Dancing Ledge

10. The main route turns briefly inland here. Follow the path slightly uphill before bearing left. Look out for a small, stone 'Coast Path' waymarker and some steps leading up to the left, towards the top of the cliffs above the quarry.

11. At the top of the steps, turn left and follow the path around the top of the quarry until it meets a kissing gate.

INFO: THE HALSEWELL

As you approach the kissing gate, you'll have great views of the steep cliffs ahead. This is the spot where the Halsewell foundered and 168 people lost their lives. With Winspit Quarry only just up the coast, it's worth reflecting on the fact that before the Halsewell broke apart, the crew fired its cannons to try and alert the local quarrymen to the disaster unfolding in the water below. Given how close the quarry is, it's testament to the ferocity of the storm that no one heard the shots.

12. After the gate, continue along the coast path for a half mile or so until you arrive above the large quarry at Winspit.

13. As the path curves to the right you'll see a gate on the left. Here, turn your back on the gate and quarry, taking the grassy track up the steep side of East Man. Your calves will be burning by the time you reach the top!

14. At the brow of the hill, follow the ridge northwards, with the quarry to your back and the village of Worth Matravers on your left. Keep to the ridge, and don't be tempted to lose height by dropping into the valley.

THE ROUTE

It's worth noting that while this path doesn't appear on OS maps, it is a public right of way. It's perfectly easy to follow, if a little muddy after heavy rainfall.

15. You'll arrive at a convergence of drystone walls where you should continue north, keeping the wall with its windswept hawthorn trees to your right until it meets the main road through the village.

LUNCH STOP?

When you reach the road, you could turn left and drop in at The Square and Compass (complete with its fossil museum) for a pint, a pasty and to take advantage of the facilities. Don't forget - there's no toilet back at the car park in Langton. See page 43 for some food and drink suggestions.

16. If you do stop in the village - retrace your steps back to where you joined the main road and continue along it, away from the village, for a few hundred yards. Take the first wooden gate on the right marked 'Public Footpath'.

17. Head across the field to a gate and cross the concrete track beyond, following the path for a half mile or so through two more fields before you reach a large wooden gate and a signpost.

18. Go through the gate and onto the Priest's Way, following the signpost to 'Langton Matravers'.

19. Continue along the Priest's Way for about a mile and a half as it wends its way past various modern quarries.

THE VIEW: As the track begins to head downhill, the Isle of Wight will be visible ahead on a clear day and, if you turn to your left, you'll see the elongated masses of Nine Barrow and Ballard Downs stretching west to east.

DETOUR: THE DINOSAURS' FOOTPRINTS
Shortly after joining the Priest's Way, keep an eye out for a gate on the left marked 'Dinosaur Footprints'. 140 million years ago, there was a shallow lagoon where you're walking. Dinosaurs used to gather here and they've left behind rather a lot of footprints! If you go through the gate, a couple of minutes' walk will bring you to Keates Quarry where you can look at the footprints and read more about them.

20. Don't be tempted to turn left until you reach the four-way sign post you passed right at the start of the walk. Take the left-hand path marked 'Langton' and follow the track back to the car park. ●

Nine Barrow Down

Corfe Castle • Ancient round barrows

Length 5 miles **Time** 1½-2 hours **Difficulty** Easy, one moderate decent on steep steps
Toilets Corfe Castle Visitor Centre **Refreshments** Many pubs in Corfe Castle village
Start & Finish NT Corfe Castle Car Park **Postcode** BH20 5DR **OS Ref** SY 959 824

A gentle amble up to Ninebarrow's namesake peak, with breath-taking vistas of Poole Harbour on the way up and equally beautiful views of Corfe Castle and its village on the way back. Keep your eyes and ears open for the famous steam engines of the Swanage Railway!

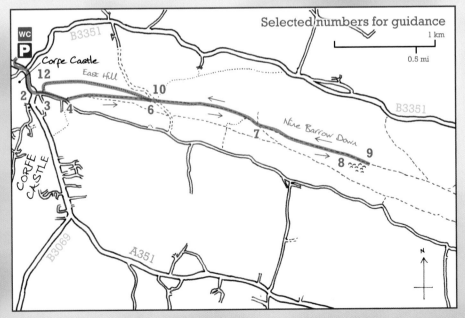

♪ Summer Fires

There's a long historical tradition across Europe of lighting bonfires on Midsummer's Day - sometimes on the high points of land around a settlement. People would leap through the fire for good luck and sometimes lead their animals around it for the same reason. We just thought the image of people jumping across the fire at dusk was such a beautiful one and that the notion of living for the moment, before the hardships of the shorter days arrive, was one we could relate to.

The real place we had in mind was the range of hills that surround the village of Corfe - one of which is our namesake hill: 'Nine Barrow Down'.

If you're looking for the perfect time of day to do this walk, it's sunset. The sun setting just to the right of the castle really is something to behold if you get it on a good day! And in fact, it was on this very spot that we imagined the people of old lighting their midsummer bonfires, hoping to usher in an autumn of bountiful harvests.

NB: These notes don't really cover the background of Corfe Castle itself – if you're looking for further info on that, see **page 67**.

•

We tend to park at the main National Trust car park in Corfe. There are parking options a little further into the village, but they're difficult to manoeuvre in and, to be honest, usually full.

1. Use the crossing outside the front of the visitor centre to cross the busy A351. Turn left, taking the pavement alongside the main road up towards the village.

2. As the road bends right into the village proper, look for Sandy Hill Lane on the opposite side of the road.

3. Take care as you re-cross the main road and follow Sandy Hill Lane underneath the railway bridge until you reach a small walkers' car park on your left.

4. Just after the car park, take the footpath on the left marked 'Purbeck Way' and make your way through the double gate and onto the track leading up the southern flank of East Hill. This 'winding track' and the fields that eventually emerge on the right are the images we had in mind when we wrote 'Summer Fires'.

5. Continue up the Ridge Path, until you eventually reach the minor blight of the radio mast at the top of the hill. We'll overlook this though, as the walk boasts more than enough good views to counteract it!

6. With the mast on your left, go through the smaller of two gates, continuing uphill along the Purbeck Way for a quarter of a mile until you pass through another gate.

7. In another quarter of a mile, you'll reach a four-way signpost. Continue straight ahead on the Purbeck Way and a final gate will lead you to a slightly steeper section of path.

THE VIEW: To the north, a vast expanse of lowland heath fills the foreground below you but, as you look out beyond the harbour to the conurbations of Poole and Bournemouth, it's hard to imagine that only a few hundred years ago, virtually everything, as far as the eye could see, would have been Thomas Hardy's heathland. Some 50,000 hectares stretched from the Avon Valley in the east, across Purbeck and all the way to Dorchester. To the south-east Swanage and its bay are visible.

8. When the path splits at the top, take the higher route to the left and within a few minutes, you should be able to see the distinctive tumuli that characterise the crest of Nine Barrow Down.

Nine Barrow Down

9. Once you've enjoyed the views (and perhaps succeeded in finding all nine of the barrows!) it's time to 'about turn'. We very rarely go in for there-and-back-again walks but we make an exception in this case. As soon as you turn around, it becomes apparent that the views on the return journey are going to be quite different - but no less glorious!

THE VIEW: As you retrace your steps, you have lovely views to the south-west. Harman's Cross is in the middle-distance and, beyond, the distant church tower of St James' in Kingston nestles below the plantation that backs on to the Encombe Estate. In the foreground, you can clearly see the village of Corfe and its own church of St Edward which also gets a mention in 'Summer Fires'. However, dominating the landscape is the dramatic ruin of Corfe Castle itself, views of which will accompany you for the remainder of the walk. The chalk ridge behind it stretches away to the west, finally meeting its end around Worbarrow Bay, some six miles away (see Walk 8).

10. Retrace your steps to the radio mast. At this point, you have a choice. **Our preferred route back will involve quite steep steps which do require some sure footing.** If this doesn't sound like your cup of tea, now's the time to take the path down to the left and retrace your steps back to the car park.

11. If you're carrying on - ignore the tracks to right and left and take the grassy ridge along the top of East Hill with the castle ahead and to the left. Go right to the brow of the hill, where you'll have excellent views of the ruins.

12. Once you've admired the view, the steps off East Hill are to the left and can be found if you orientate yourself towards the village church. Head in this direction until you spot a stone waymarker just ahead and slightly down the hill. This marks the start of the steps which take you back down to the road, under the railway bridge, then right, back on to the main road and down to the car park. ●

FANCY A PINT?

If you fancy stopping in the village of Corfe Castle for a pint, **The Bankes Arms** is a nice place in which to huddle up on a cold day, while **The Greyhound** has the benefit of a beer garden with spectacular views of the castle above it if the weather is warmer!

The view from the Bankes Arms beer garden
Over the rooftops towards the castle

Walk Five

Worth Matravers

St. Aldhelm's Chapel • The Square & Compass

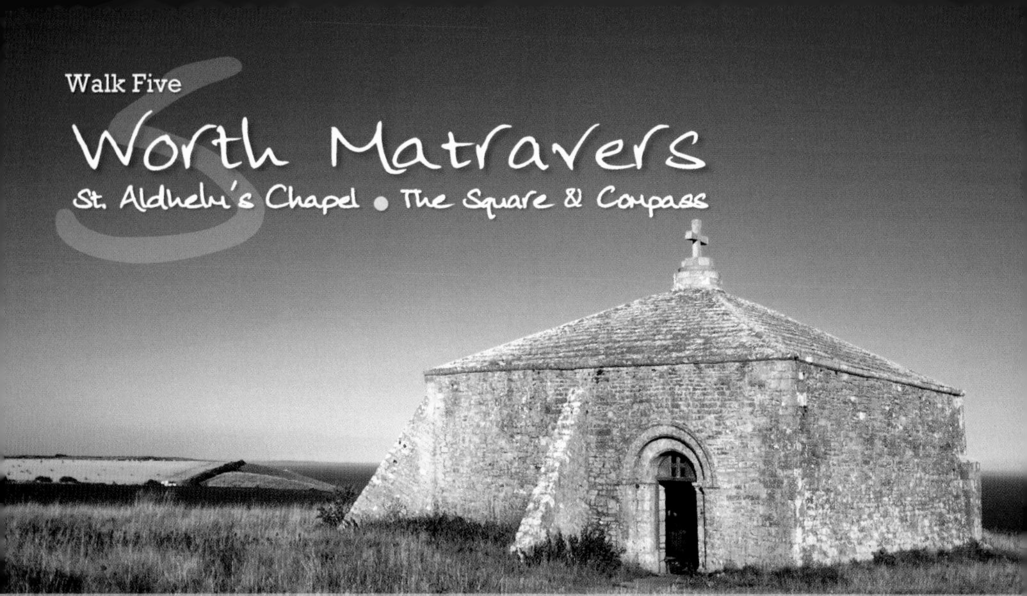

Length 5 miles **Time** 2-3 hours **Difficulty** Moderate (with some very steep steps, up & down)
Toilets Worth Matravers Car Park **Refreshments** The Square & Compass, Worth Matravers
Start & Finish Worth Matravers Car Park **Postcode** BH19 3LQ **OS Ref** SY 974 777

Without a doubt one of our favourite walks, taking in a charming 12th century chapel right out on the clifftop. The views as you approach the coastline are simply incredible!

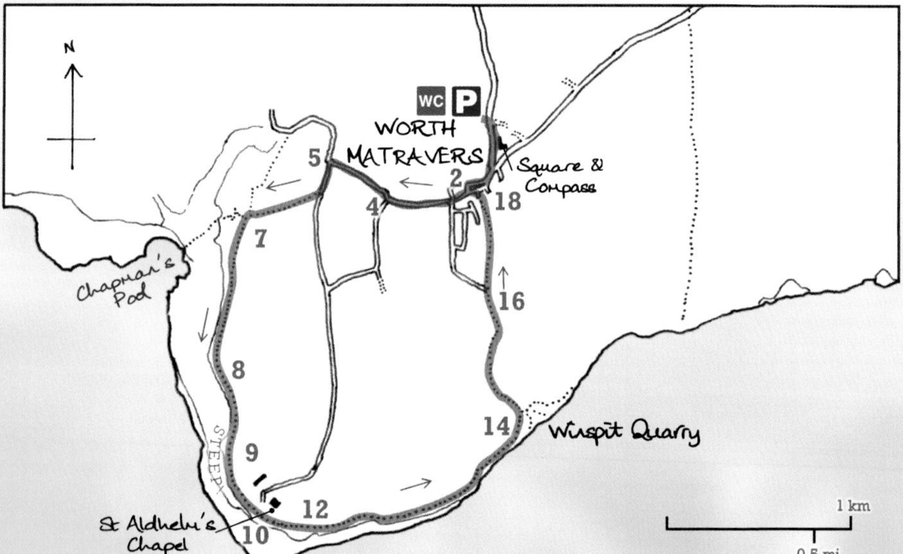

Selected numbers for guidance

♪ The Pinner

There's a shelf in our house that's absolutely crammed with books on Dorset folklore. In one, we discovered a lovely bit of history relating to a place that's been a feature of many good coastal walks over the years: St Aldhelm's Chapel, near Worth Matravers, right on the South Coast. This exquisite little chapel dates right back to the twelfth century.

The book tells how women would place trinkets, particularly pins, in the central pillar of the chapel whilst wishing for their heart's desire. Sure enough, the next time we visited the chapel, there in the pillar, we saw the flashes of blue, where the copper in old pins was slowly oxidising.

We just thought it was a lovely image - and 'The Pinner' is about a woman who toils her whole life to make the perfect pin. She believes that if she can produce one that is completely flawless, her wish will be granted.

There are a number of places to park in Worth Matravers, but the main car park benefits from public toilets, as well as easy access to the Square & Compass pub at the end of the walk!

•

1. Turn right out of the car park and head down-hill past the pub.

2. At the bottom of the hill turn right, and keep right, walking up through the village with the pond on your left. Snake through the village, passing St Nicholas' Church on your right, and stay on the road as it exits the village.

3. Follow the road until you reach Weston Farm.

THE VIEW: As you leave the village, rolling fields begin to unfold to the south, with a gentle valley leading down to Winspit. To the south-east you'll be able to spot the old medieval strip farming 'lynchets' on the flanks of East Man and West Man (further info on 'lynchets' can be found on page 51). One of the last surviving groups of the open field system in Dorset, these were no doubt associated with the medieval Manor at Worth Matravers. To the south-west, you'll already be able to see the coastguard cottages and St Aldhelm's chapel - the main destination of this walk.

4. Following the sign to 'Car Park', continue on the road as it curves to the right and then to the left. Continue along the road with open fields on either side (note the field study centre on the right - we'll discuss this more later!).

5. At the end of the road turn left, and take the stony track to the car park on your right. At the far end of the car park, pass through the gate.

6. Follow the path westwards through two fields, until you reach a hedgerow and stile. Climb over onto the side of West Hill.

THE VIEW: As you climb over, the side of West Hill will drop away steeply below, only for the land to rise up again in the form of Houns Tout Cliff (the latter part pronounced 'toot', as it relates to the Middle English word 'tute' meaning 'look out'). The grey Kimmeridge Clay of the cliffs slumps down towards **Chapman's Pool** and if you look south-west, Portland Bill sits atop the horizon if the visibility is clear.

Chapman's Pool

7. Turn left and follow the track southwards, with a dry-stone wall to your left.

INFO: CHAPMAN'S POOL LIFEBOAT STATION
If you feel like venturing a little to the right for a better view of Chapman's Pool - take care. However, you should be able to see, far below, what looks like a little fishing hut. This is precisely what it is now - although previously it was the Chapman's Pool lifeboat station. Built in response to the large number of lives lost at sea in the local area, it was finished in 1867 but operated only until 1880. Constant landslips made its upkeep very costly and, without a village close-by, too few volunteers were available to man it.

THE VIEW: The coastline to the west begins to open up and, in good visibility, offers views of numerous headlands: first Egmont Point, then Rope Lake Head, Broad Bench and finally Worbarrow Tout, with the white cliffs of Worbarrow Bay behind it. It becomes more indistinct beyond there, as the coast continues towards Lulworth.

Radar Memorial

A memorial sculpture commemorating the radar research carried out at Worth Matravers between 1940 and 1942.

8. You'll pass the Emmett's Hill memorial garden on your left. Built by the Royal Marines Association, it commemorates marines killed in conflicts between 1945 and 1990, although a new stone was added in 2005 to commemorate those lost in more recent conflicts. Moving on, climb over the stile and continue along the track.

9. The path will lead to the top of a rather steep set of steps leading down into the valley below. We call this part of the walk 'the up-down', although having reflected on this, 'the 'down-up' would probably be a better description, as this is exactly what you now need to do! We've never counted how many steps go down the northern side as it never seems important, however we can tell you that there are 218 going up the southern side. You seem to have more time to ponder these things on the slow climb upwards!

10. At the top, take the opportunity to catch your breath on the stone bench and admire the hard-won view before heading towards the chapel.

INFO: THE PINNER

If you have a torch, or light on your phone, you should easily be able to see the holes in the central pillar and, inside, traces of the trinkets left over the centuries by girls and women using this as a 'wishing chapel'. You might even find the odd bee hibernating in there depending on the time of year. A visit during the summer will often reward with a display of martins flying at high speed around the building, diving in and out of the open door.

11. Head out of the chapel and down to the coastguard station and the radar memorial sculpture beyond it.

INFO: RADAR TOWERS

On this part of the walk, keep an eye out for overgrown concrete Radar Towers beneath your feet. There are a number of old foundations left on the cliffs around this area and they were the sites of **radar towers**. From May 1940 to May 1942, Worth Matravers was the centre for radar research in the UK, and the technology developed here was decisive in the eventual allied victory in the Second World War. Other than these foundations, the only other remnant of 'RAF Worth Matravers' is the field study hut that you passed earlier on in the walk. The actual sign for RAF Worth Matravers can now be seen hanging behind the door in the Square and Compass pub.

12. Continue along the coast path and you'll shortly come to an abandoned quarry on the right. It's worth exploring a little! Out on the cliff edge you'll find a precariously balanced stone monolith left behind by the old quarry workers.

13. Continue along the coast path, following it for about half a mile until you reach the disused quarry of Winspit. Note that the path can get quite slippery here after prolonged wet weather.

THE VIEW:

You'll now have views along the eastern coast - Seacombe, Dancing Ledge and the many cliffs and caves beyond, eventually leading to Anvil Point, where you'll be able to spot the white outline of Anvil Point Lighthouse, operational since 1881. Automated in 1991 and now equipped with an LED lamp, it is still in use today.

14. The path will curve around the top of the quarry taking you slightly inland before reaching some steps which lead down to the old quarry track. Turn right to go and explore the quarry.

INFO: WINSPIT QUARRY

Winspit Until around 1940, **Winspit** was an active quarry. Indeed, the Purbeck Stone sought there and elsewhere in the Isle of Purbeck has been quarried since Roman times. Purbeck Stone has been used in high profile buildings in London and beyond, including St Paul's Cathedral. The old cottage, buildings and caves are well worth exploring - and you can certainly see why the location has been popular for film sets, including Doctor Who, where it was used as an abandoned Dalek city!

15. Once you've explored the quarry, retrace your route out of it and back to the bottom of the steps, passing them on your left and heading north up the track towards Worth Matravers.

16. When the track forks, take the right-hand path, with the water treatment plant to your left. Continue uphill until you reach a gate.

17. With cottages on your left, turn right and up into the village with the phone box and pond to your left.

18. As you approach The Square and Compass, you could turn left up the hill and back to the car park. However, we can assure you that the far better option is to head to the pub. It's even got its own fossil museum! Grab a pie (cheese and veg is our personal favourite) and a pint (Hattie Browns 'Moonlight' is a regular and very good) and sit and enjoy the view. You've earned it! ●

The Square & Compass beer garden
Taken in the autumn with its annual pumpkin display

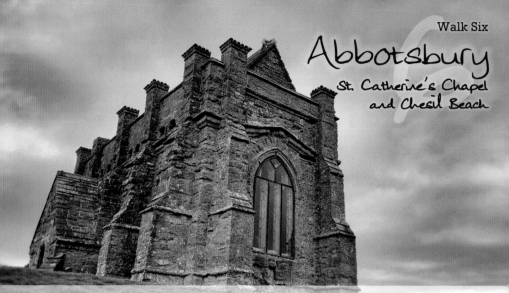

Abbotsbury

St. Catherine's Chapel and Chesil Beach

Length 6½ miles **Time** 3-4 hours **Difficulty** Moderate
Toilets Back Street, Abbotsbury **Refreshments** Many pubs and tea rooms in the village
Start & Finish Car Park off Rodden Row **Postcode** DT3 4JL **OS Ref** SY 578 853

Walking along the South Dorset Ridgeway, it's easy to see why people have been drawn to this magical area for millennia. The route back also takes in St Catherine's Chapel, via the world-famous Chesil Beach, a UNESCO World Heritage Site.

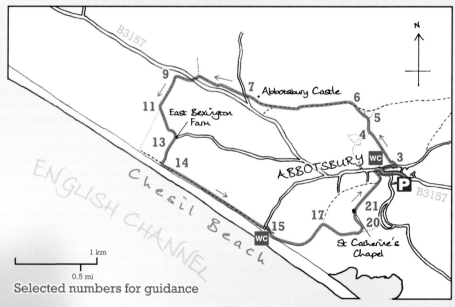

Selected numbers for guidance

♪ Overthrown

Like 'To the Stones', 'Overthrown' was also inspired by the South Dorset Ridgeway. Humanity has been drawn to this enigmatic landscape for thousands of years - scattering hillforts, henges, burial mounds and monuments across the Ridgeway's 17-mile length (for more information, see the QR code on page 51). Today, modern humans still make their impact on the landscape: building settlements, farms and roads to serve the thrumming demands of our modern society.

But in this song, we imagine the Ridgeway set at some point in the future, when mankind is no longer the master of this landscape. As the scars of our impact on the hills and vales start to heal, the grass and wildflowers of the Ridgeway begin to transform it back into the untamed and beautiful place it once was.

You'll find the main car park on the eastern side of the village of Abbotsbury, just off the B3157. The charges are pretty reasonable but it is also sometimes possible to find on-street parking in the village. There's plenty to do in Abbotsbury, so make sure you leave time to visit the many galleries and, of course, the famous Swannery.

1. Assuming you do park in the main car park, head left out of it, make your way down the main road and turn right onto Market Street.

2. Turn right onto Back Street (opposite the Ilchester Arms) and continue up this road until you reach a footpath on the left, just before 'Spring Cottage'.

Two little doves
inside St Catherine's Chapel

45

Ridgeway Brazier
Looking along Chesil Beach towards the Isle of Portland

3. At the signpost, follow the path uphill to 'Blind Lane', 'Hillfort' & 'Hardy Monument'. The enclosed track will gradually open up giving you some views of Abbotsbury below.

4. Continue through a gate and upwards until the 3-way sign post. Take the north-westerly sign towards 'Abbotsbury Hillfort'.

5. After another gate, the path opens out into tiered fields. Continue upwards towards a gate below a small rocky outcrop. Continue to follow signs to Abbotsbury Hillfort (referred to on OS maps as 'Abbotsbury Castle') until the next gate, where you will join the South Dorset Ridgeway.

6. Take the Ridgeway westward, with the coast to your left. After just over half a mile, you'll pass an old beacon and what we assume is a stone pillbox on your left.

THE VIEW: In the far west, across the county boundary and into Devon, you can see the red cliffs of Sidmouth - the site of a very fine folk festival!

7. Stay on The Ridgeway until you reach the road, going through the gate and crossing straight over. Follow the gravel path up out of the informal parking spots and stay on it until steps lead you to a triangulation pillar just within the 'ramparts' of Abbotsbury Castle.

THE VIEW: Hardy Monument is to the east (see Walk 7, Page 52).

INFO:
ABBOTSBURY CASTLE

Abbotsbury Castle

You might be forgiven for expecting something a little more 'fortified' from the title 'castle', but this Iron Age hillfort was once the frontline of defence against the Romans. However, when the Romans did invade in AD43, it didn't prove too difficult for them to take this particular castle. Afterwards, they moved swiftly inland towards Maiden Castle near Dorchester.

8. Continue over the western ramparts of the fort and straight ahead to where the path is joined by a drystone wall. Cross the road and follow signs for West Bexington.

9. Go through a kissing gate and follow the wall. Continue to follow it as it bends 90 degrees to the left. Follow markers to Chesil Beach as the path goes steeply downhill for a quarter of a mile.

10. At the 3-way sign, take the left route to East Bexington and Chesil Beach. Take the stile and follow the hedgerow downhill, bearing left at the bottom to access another stile.

11. Climb over and follow the path diagonally southwards towards East Bexington Farm.

12. Turn left onto the public footpath through the farm, keeping the buildings to your right as the path curves around.

13. When you meet the main track leading towards the farmhouse buildings, cut across it and downhill through a gate into the final field before the beach. Follow the hedgerow on the right to the bottom of the field and turn left onto a tarmac road.

14. Continue along the road for about a mile, looking out for WW2 pillboxes on either side, until you reach a car park and toilets.

Chesil Beach

INFO: CHESIL BEACH

Chesil Beach is one of three major shingle structures in Britain. Some 18 miles long, it connects the Isle of Portland with the mainland and is, in places, 660 feet wide and 50 feet high. The tidal lagoon behind the beach is called The Fleet, and together these features have been designated a UNESCO World Heritage Site.

15. Walk through the car park and cut to the right and onto the back of the shingle for a few hundred yards until you see a stone waymarker for the 'Coast Path' and 'Abbotsbury'.

16. Follow the path as it soon curves left and towards St Catherine's Chapel. Continue following the 'Coast Path'; the chapel will disappear below the treeline for a time.

17. At the 3-way sign, take the 'Swannery' route. Climb over the stile and take the path uphill past a pillbox.

18. Pass a wall on your right running downhill and continue to a wall on your left running up the hill. Go through the gate.

INFO:
WW2 & THE BOUNCING BOMB

Bouncing Bombs

If you look south from here, you'll be able to see a line of concrete blocks running across the beach. These are 'dragon's teeth' anti-tank defences (similar to those in Walk 8 around Tyneham) and are yet another reminder that the Dorset coast was a very likely target in the event of Nazi invasion during the Second World War. However, the area also had a more 'offensive' application as well. Not only was the beach used as a place to train machine gunners, but Barnes Wallis also tested the Dambusters' bouncing bomb on the waters of The Fleet.

The view from Abbotsbury Castle
Looking towards Devon

19. After the gate, cut up the hill diagonally away from the wall. As the path curves to the right, you'll soon have the wall directly to your back.

20. Keep an eye out for a pillbox below you on the right. Above it, the path forks. Take the left-hand route, following an indistinct path towards the top of the hill and St Catherine's Chapel.

21. From the Chapel, follow a grass track down towards the village. This path eventually becomes gravel and takes you through two gates. When you reach the main road, turn right and continue through the village and back to the car park. ●

INFO:
ST. CATHERINE'S CHAPEL

St Catherine's Chapel

Although no documents exist which record exactly when the chapel was built, its style dates to the late 14th Century – the same as Abbotsbury Abbey in the village below. It is thought that it was built as a retreat and place of pilgrimage for the monks of the Abbey. Whilst the Abbey was destroyed during Henry VIII's dissolution of the monasteries, the chapel was spared, probably because of its usefulness as a coastal beacon. It is now under the care of English Heritage, but is often open to the public and admission is free.

The Grey Mare and her Colts

Neolithic Longbarrow ● Kingston Russell Stone Circle

Length 4½ miles **Time** 2½-3 hours **Difficulty** Moderate
Toilets and Refreshments None on the walk, nearest in Abbotsbury village
Start & Finish Bishop's Lime Kiln, Bishops Rd **Postcode** DT3 4JW* (See map) **OS Ref** SY 587 858

A walk through an ancient land of bone and stone, visiting a historic long barrow and a mysterious, Bronze Age stone circle - with magnificent views along the West Dorset Heritage Coast

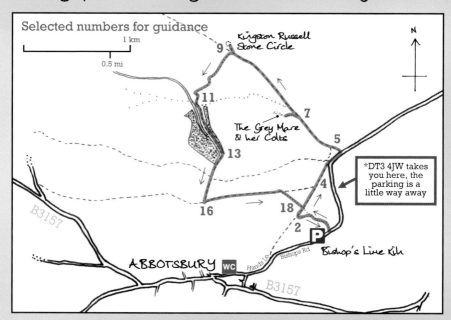

Selected numbers for guidance

1 km

0.5 mi

N

9 Kingston Russell Stone Circle

11

The Grey Mare & her Colts

7

5

13

4

*DT3 4JW takes you here, the parking is a little way away

16

18

2

P Bishop's Lime Kiln

ABBOTSBURY WC

Hands Ln

Bishops Rd

B3157

B3157

♪ To the Stones

We have a fantastic organisation called 'Dorset Artsreach' in our neck of the woods which brings the arts to many rural locations around the county. They were part of a project called 'The Land of Bone and Stone', designed to raise awareness of the rich archaeological heritage of the South Dorset Ridgeway - a 17-mile stretch of chalk downland. We were commissioned to write a series of songs that would highlight and celebrate this amazing ceremonial landscape.

The Ridgeway

'To the Stones' was inspired by a Neolithic long barrow called 'The Grey Mare and her Colts' on the Ridgeway just above Abbotsbury. It tells of a family taking their child up to this important monument for the first time. Not simply a house for the dead, it's introduced to the child as an integral part of the community, where they will be able to find spiritual strength and support throughout their lives.

The parking spot for this walk is a place called 'Bishop's Lime Kiln'. You reach it by following the minor road north-east out of Abbotsbury for about a mile. The car park is on the left. At the back of it is...well...a lime kiln! We haven't really been able to find out anything else about it, but it was presumably once used to make quicklime for agricultural use.

1. Walk out onto the road, turning left up the hill for 10 yards or so, before turning immediately left onto a track that leads to a metal gate and wooden signpost. Climb the stile adjacent to the gate and head west for approximately 300 yards, keeping the slope of the field's higher tier directly to your right.

THE VIEW: To the south-east is the bulky western side of the Isle of Portland; south-west is Abbotsbury and St Catherine's Chapel; directly south is Chesil Beach (all of which are discussed in greater detail in Walk 6).

INFO: MEDIEVAL LYNCHETS

Medieval Lynchets

The fields here are strangely tiered due to their historic agricultural use. These wide strip farming 'lynchets' probably date to the Medieval period. There is some debate as to whether they were dug or formed naturally as sections of the hillside were ploughed repeatedly - but either way - they make for an interesting hillside!

2. After passing four small hawthorn trees in quick succession on your right, the field's higher tier converges with the level on which you've been walking. At this point, turn right and follow a sunken track north-east up the hill, with Chesil Beach to your back.

3. At the top of this track, continue uphill and through a gate for another couple of hundred yards.

THE VIEW: On the skyline to the north-east a tower rises up above Black Down. Built in 1844, this 72-foot structure is **'Hardy Monument'**. Not, as many believe, a monument to the writer Thomas Hardy, but rather, to the slightly less well-known Vice Admiral Sir Thomas Hardy. He was a naval officer and, most notably, the man in whose arms Admiral Lord Nelson died at the Battle of Trafalgar, after uttering the now famous words, 'kiss me Hardy'.

4. Continue in the same direction, through two more gates, following signs to the South Dorset Ridgeway until you emerge onto a road. Head up the hill and in a few hundred yards, turn left at a signpost to 'The Grey Mare and her Colts' and continue until you reach some gravelly parking spots in front of the entrance to Gorwell Farm.

5. There's a gravel track here on the right. Go onto it, but rather than following it as it curves to the right, go straight ahead through a metal gate (marked with an English Heritage arrow) and onto the public bridleway between a hedgerow on the left and a field fence on the right. Follow this in a north-westerly direction, for a third of a mile.

6. Just after you pass a metal gate on your right, you'll spot a stile on the left. Climb over and follow the field boundary fence on the left-hand side until, in a few hundred yards, you meet a gate on your left.

7. Through the gate and to the left, you'll find the Neolithic long barrow and subject of 'To The Stones': The Grey Mare and her Colts. Two upright stones still survive at the southern end of the barrow, though the burial chamber collapsed long ago.

8. Retrace your steps back to the stile and continue north-west along the track for another half mile where you'll find the Kingston Russell Stone Circle on your right.

INFO: KINGSTON RUSSELL STONE CIRCLE

Stone Circle It's a shame that the stones are no longer standing, but the site is in fact the largest of the nine surviving stone circles in Dorset. It's believed that it dates to the Neolithic period or perhaps the early Bronze Age.

9. Return to the track and to the five-way signpost. Cross the track to the gate opposite the signpost and follow the blue arrow south-west through a gate.

10. Follow the hedgerow on your left downhill into the valley, until you meet a gate at the bottom of the hill.

11. After the gate, continue downhill with the houses on your left, joining the Gorwell Farm track.

12. On meeting the track, turn left and go through another gate, joining the tarmac road and passing farm buildings on either side.

13. Leaving the farm complex behind you, continue on up this road until a concrete track presents itself on your right.

14. Take this track and, at the top, continue straight ahead and through a gate onto a public bridleway between the two fields.

15. Go through the next gate and immediately through another gate on your left, before continuing south, with the fence to your right.

16. When the fence meets a gate, rather than going through the gate, turn left, keeping the fencing to your right.

THE VIEW: Here the views of Chesil Beach, Portland and St Catherine's Chapel open up again, and the crumbling remains of Abbotsbury Abbey can also be seen with its huge tithe barn. You can nip through the gate to a stone bench to get the very best views before returning to the path.

17. Continue along the path to the east. In about three quarters of a mile, you'll reach the same sunken path that you came up at the beginning of the walk.

18. Re-trace your steps down the sunken path and back to the field level on which you began the walk.

19. Head to the lower lynchet, turning left and heading due east until you see the signpost at the edge of the Lime Kiln coppice. Climbing the stile will bring you back down to the car park. ●

Tyneham

Historic village ruins • Worbarrow Bay

Length 4½ miles **Time** 2-3 hours **Difficulty** Moderate-Hard (with one very steep climb)
Toilets Tyneham Visitor Centre **Refreshments** None nearby
Start & Finish Tyneham Village Car Park **Postcode** '"Tyneham, Wareham" **OS Ref** SY 883 802

The 'lost village' of Tyneham has been within an army firing range since the second world war. Fortunately, this time capsule and the beautiful surrounding landscape can be still be explored and enjoyed.

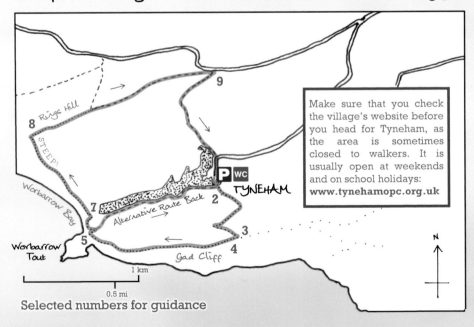

Make sure that you check the village's website before you head for Tyneham, as the area is sometimes closed to walkers. It is usually open at weekends and on school holidays: **www.tynehamopc.org.uk**

Selected numbers for guidance

♪ For a Time

Tyneham Village can be found nestling in a secluded valley, not far from Lulworth on the South coast of Dorset. During the Second World War it was commandeered by The War Office to be used for the D-Day preparations. The villagers were moved out of Tyneham and scattered to various dwellings around the Isle of Purbeck.

They were willing to do their duty and play their part in the war effort on the understanding that, when the war was over, they would be able to return to their homes. They were never allowed back. To this day, the village is still owned by the Ministry of Defence and is now part of the Lulworth firing ranges.

The song is a fictional encounter between a visitor to the village and one of the former residents. As he explains the story of the abandoned village, the elderly man reminds the visitor to appreciate the freedom that was bought by the sacrifices of so many. Given humanity's propensity for making the same mistakes again and again, the visitor is left with the rather sobering thought that we should all make the best of the peace time, fragile as it is.

There is a large car park for visitors to the village (suggested donation of £2). It goes without saying that before or after your walk you should take time to go and explore this most extraordinary piece of Dorset history. We shan't describe it here as part of the walk. It's got many nooks and crannies - many secrets - and it's well worth taking the time and to enjoy discovering them for yourself.

1. From the Tyneham car park, take the road southwards away from the village, through the gate and over the bridge.

2. Pass the toilets on the left, go straight ahead through a gate and follow the path between the yellow markers as it zig-zags to the top of the hill.

IMPORTANT INFO: YELLOW MARKERS & GIANT NUMBERS

You'll be able to spot yellow markers either side of a path snaking up the side of Gold Down ahead. You'll no doubt have noticed from all the 'Military Firing Range' notices that it's really important that you stay between these markers throughout the course of this walk to make sure you don't stumble across any unexploded ordnance! You'll no doubt also have spotted the giant number 7 on the hillside. There are a variety of numbers scattered throughout the valley to aid the target practice which takes place by the army when people aren't enjoying the range walks.

THE VIEW: As you gain height, you'll be turned to the west for a time and will be rewarded with some impressive views of the white chalk cliffs towering above Worbarrow and Mupe Bays. Rings Hill, topped with Flowers Barrow, rises steeply above them, forming the highest point on the other side of the valley.

3. Turn right immediately after the path takes you through a large metal gate and head to the top of the hill. When you're nearly at the brow of the hill, turn right through the wooden gate and onto the top of Gad Cliff.

THE VIEW: For much of the route along the ridge, you won't be able to see back along the coast to the south-east, as the Portland Stone of Gad Cliff will block your view. However, at this point, where the grass is short, it's worth (carefully) poking your head up to take in views as the coast stretches first past Brandy Bay, then Hobarrow Bay, on to Kimmeridge Bay and finally to the Kimmeridge ledges beyond. In the far distance is St Aldhelm's Head, with its coast guard cottages and chapel visible on a clear day (see Walk 5).

4. Take the path west towards Worbarrow Bay until it begins to descend to the right. Follow the path down towards the valley floor.

THE VIEW. On the far side of the valley, the slumping cliffs below Rings Hill become clearer the further you progress. So too the Mupe Ledges and Mupe Rocks as they jut back westward into the bay. As the path begins to descend, the prominent rock outcrop of Worbarrow Tout separates the main bay from Pondfield Cove on its eastern side (for an explanation of the word 'tout' see page 38). It is this smaller cove that really becomes the visual focus as you descend, its cliff wall showing off some of the Jurassic Coast's

Purbeck Geology wonderfully complex geology. But beside the cliffs you'll spot a more modern rock structure in the form the concrete 'Dragon's Teeth' anti-tank defences - just one of several Second World War relics visible during the course of this walk.

5. Once off Gold Down, do go and explore Pondfield Cove to the left, before doing the same on the other side of the Tout with Worbarrow Bay.

6. When you're ready, you'll be following the signs to the 'South West Coast Path'. But before you turn west off the main track and up the other side of the valley, continue inland for a few metres and turn to your left next to the flag pole to see an almost fully intact 'Allan Williams' gun turret.

INFO: ALLAN WILLIAMS GUN TURRET

Allan Williams Turret

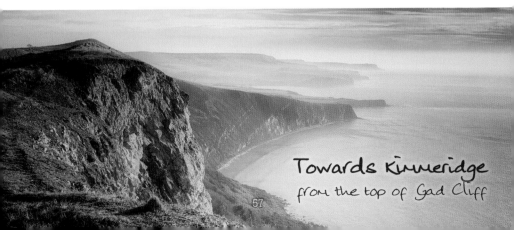

These were designed to house one man and to rotate 360 degrees. Not somewhere one would have probably enjoyed being stationed in the event of a Nazi invasion!

ALTERNATIVE ROUTE:

It is worth saying that if you don't fancy the look of the climb up the other side of the valley, it is possible to simply take the main path out of Worbarrow Bay and follow it all the way back to Tyneham Village and the main car park.

7. Retrace your steps and take the coast path up the steep track leading to the top of Rings Hill, passing a number of WW2 pill-boxes on the way. It's a bit of a slog, but the views are well worth it! When you reach the top, go through the gate and directly ahead onto Flowers Barrow.

THE VIEW:

At the top of Rings Hill, you'll find what remains of 'Flower's Barrow' - an iron age hillfort. Surely there can't be many hillforts with more beautiful views than this?! In another example of the amazing geology at work in the Isle of Purbeck, you're actually standing on the western end of the chalk ridge that extends all the way to Ballard Down above Swanage (covered in more detail in Walk 1). In fact, the chalk ridge once extended all the way to the Isle of Wight before rising sea levels separated it from the mainland. To the north-west, you should be able to spot Lulworth Castle in the middle distance.

INFO: LULWORTH CASTLE

Lulworth Castle

Lulworth Castle is actually a mock castle, having been completed in the early 17th Century and built in the style of those constructed in the Middle-Ages.

Towards Kimmeridge
from the top of Gad Cliff

8. When you've rested and absorbed the view, take the path to the east and along the top of the ridge until you reach a triangulation pillar in about a mile.

THE VIEW: Povington Heath and the army ranges stretch out to your left, while the secluded Tyneham valley now nestles to your right.

9. Just before you reach the road, the path turns sharply to the right. Follow it back down the valley side, into the village of Tyneham and back to the car park. ●

The view from Flowers Barrow
Towards Worbarrow Bay and Worbarrow Tout

Walk Nine

Osmington

Osmington White Horse
Bincombe Bumps

Length 5 miles **Time** 2-3 hours **Difficulty** Moderate
Toilets & Refreshments The Springhead, Sutton Poyntz
Start & Finish Church Lane, Osmington **Postcode** DT3 6EW **OS Ref** SY 723 835

A wonderful ridgeway walk, with views of the mysterious barrows of the Bincombe Bumps, the iconic Osmington White Horse and the Isle of Portland due south.

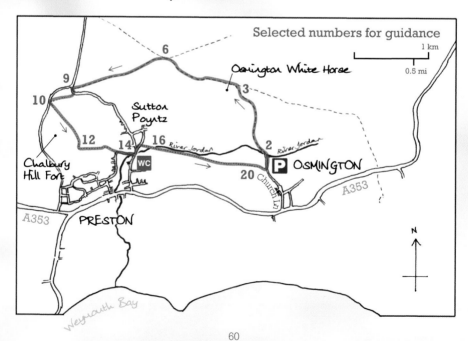

♪ Mother

Just outside Weymouth you'll find Bincombe Hill, atop which there are six burial mounds. According to local folklore, should someone stray too close, they might be able to hear the lilting strains of music, produced by the fairy folk who live within.

'Mother' is the story of a child who hears this music and is stolen by fairies. In our tale, the girl's mother attempts to break the fairy magic by burning thorns on top of one of the mounds, lest her child's soul be sold to hell. This is the third song in our 'Land of Bone and Stone' collection. For more information on the South Dorset Ridgeway, see the QR code on page 51.

This walk won't quite get you close enough to the 'bumps' to hear the fairy music, but it does have some pretty good views! The best parking can be found right at the end of Church Lane, which you can reach by turning off the A353 into Osmington and heading as far north through the village as you can go. Park up just before the tarmac ends.

1. Walk downhill to the end of Church Lane and when you see a signpost saying 'Bincombe 3 miles', continue onto a rocky track.

THE VIEW: As you pass some breaks in the left-hand hedgerow, you'll catch some oblique glimpses of the Osmington White Horse to your left. You'll get far better views of this towards the end of the walk!

2. The path curves to the right before passing through a gate. It then turns left, heading up the side of White Horse Hill

The view from White Horse Hill
down towards Weymouth and Portland

3. Towards the top of the track, the path splits and you should take the left-hand fork which leads through a gate and westwards. Follow signs to Bincombe.

THE VIEW: To the south-west the coast stretches towards Weymouth and the Isle of Portland – Dorset's southernmost point. The straight lines of Portland Harbour's concrete groynes and breakwaters provide a stark contrast to the rolling hills and winding coastline around it. When it was finished in 1872 it was the world's largest man-made harbour and still ranks third today.

Portland Harbour

4. After a few hundred yards of open grass, go through the gate ahead and the path will become more well-defined with a fence to the left and a hedgerow to the right. You'll pass an Ordnance Survey triangulation pillar in the field on your left.

5. As you continue along the Ridgeway, the 'Bincombe Bumps' will appear on the skyline directly to the west. There are six, though the three on the right cluster together making them slightly harder to count!

6. When you reach a three-way signpost, take the route marked 'Bincombe' and head through the gate and straight ahead into the next field.

7. A hundred yards or so ahead there's a large round barrow in the middle of the field. Pass to the left of it and follow the path as it bears left and takes you south-west through another gate.

8. Follow the path until the 'Bincombe Bumps' emerge into view again; you will also be able to see the Iron Age bulk of Chalbury Hillfort ahead and slightly to the left. Continue west until you meet the road in about half a mile.

9. Turn left onto the road and, almost immediately, you'll see a stile on the right. Climb over this, and the one directly after it, and follow the path straight ahead to the road beyond.

ALTERNATIVE ROUTE: It's worth mentioning that nettles can grow quite high along this path and, if you're wearing shorts, there is an alternative route. After point 8, turn right and walk along the road as far as the junction. Turn left and continue to follow this road for 300 yards or so around the northern side of Green Hill. Look out for a signpost to Sutton Poyntz on the left and continue from point 10.

10. When you reach the road again, take the route on the left signposted to Sutton Poyntz. Climb the stile and head south-east across the field.

11. Keeping the 'ramparts' of the hillfort on your right, continue down the hill, with Sutton Poyntz directly ahead. Pass through a gate, across the next field and through another gate.

12. After the second gate, a tall hedgerow will block views to the east. Take the path alongside the hedge as it turns 90 degrees to the left, pass through a gate and onto a path leading through the middle of the next field.

13. Follow the path out of the field and into the woodland on the other side. At the next gate, turn left on to a gravel road which doglegs right, then left, before becoming tarmac. Continue until you meet the main road.

14. First turn left, and then take the next right which is signposted to the 'Springhead Pub'. Look for the sign to the public footpath on the right and follow the path as it winds along behind the houses, before emerging back out into fields.

15. As the path winds into the next field, continue across it and through a gate which leads you to a farm track.

INFO: THE WHITE HORSE

The White Horse

The horse was cut into the hillside in 1807 and represents King George III, who was a regular visitor to the area.

16. Cross the track and continue through the next field and through another gate.

17. The path ahead is a little indistinct, but just about visible. Follow it to the north-east corner of the field (ahead and to the left) and you'll find a stile hidden just beyond the field boundary, almost within the hedge.

18. Cross into the next field and follow the fence line on your right until the next stile.

19. Climb over and cross another farm track, climbing the stile ahead of you into the next field.

20. Once again, follow the fence on your right until you reach the final stile.

21. Climb over, go through a gate and out onto a gravel track. Continuing straight ahead along the path will bring you out onto Church Lane. Assuming you parked at the end, turning left here will bring you back out to where you began. ●

A rare snowy scene
From the path along Smedmore Hill
looking out over Kimmeridge (see Walk 10)

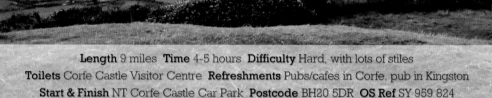

Corfe and Kimmeridge

Corfe Castle ● Kimmeridge ● Swyre Head

Length 9 miles **Time** 4-5 hours **Difficulty** Hard, with lots of stiles
Toilets Corfe Castle Visitor Centre **Refreshments** Pubs/cafes in Corfe, pub in Kingston
Start & Finish NT Corfe Castle Car Park **Postcode** BH20 5DR **OS Ref** SY 959 824

This walk delivers all of the magic of the Isle of Purbeck: its castle
and coastline, its farms and follies. It's the longest walk in this book,
but make a day of it. You will not be disappointed!

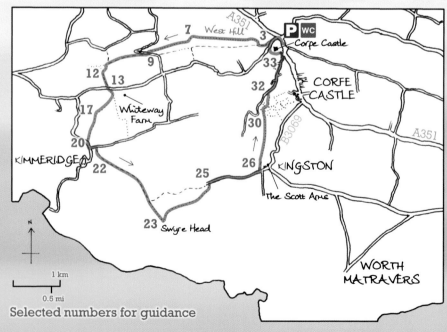

Selected numbers for guidance

♪ Siege

'Siege' is another song inspired by the beautiful and historic village of Corfe Castle. During the English Civil War, the castle was left in the hands of Lady Bankes, while her husband fought for the King. She was left with only five soldiers, four cannon and her serving women. Clearly this was not a huge force with which to defend the castle!

Hearing of this, the Parliamentarians initially sent forty men to 'relieve' the castle of its artillery – but to their surprise, Lady Bankes and her serving women managed to mount and fire one of the cannon down at them. The besieging soldiers decided that discretion was the better part of valour and that they would return another day! Later, another much larger force besieged the castle once more. While Lady Bankes managed to hold out for twenty months, she was eventually betrayed by one of her own men who let the enemy enter in the dead of night.

Our song can't really be described as historically accurate – but it's certainly inspired by Lady Bankes' spirit of defiance atop the castle walls.

INFO: CORFE CASTLE

Whilst our song about Corfe Castle is inspired by 17th century Corfe Castle events, construction of the stone keep in fact began in the early 12th century under King Henry I, son of William the Conqueror. Prior to this, the castle buildings would have been made of wood, and it's possible that Corfe's use as a defensive site goes all the way back to Roman times. Two forks of the Corfe River, the Wicken Stream and the Byle Brook, are responsible for cutting the 'motte' out of the Purbeck ridge on which the castle sits, and indeed, the word Corfe derives from the Old English 'ceorfan', meaning 'a cutting'.

As with Walk 4, the easiest place to park is the National Trust car park on the main road into the village.

1. Use the crossing outside the front of the visitor centre to cross the busy A351, and take the gate opposite signposted towards 'The Purbeck Way'.

2. Follow the path above the Corfe River until you emerge from the trees.

3. Follow the sign to 'The Rings', passing through one wooden gate, and then taking the gate immediately on your right. With the castle directly to your back, start the steep climb up West Hill. You'll soon spot some steps; follow them until they peter out.

4. Pass through one gate and then head towards another at the top of the hill. Don't go through this one though.

THE VIEW: From the top of West Hill you've got almost panoramic views. Most prominently, there is the castle itself, with East Hill behind it stretching out and becoming Nine Barrow Down. Much of this walk's route can be seen from here: to the south-west, is the chalk ridge running from Kimmeridge to Swyre Head and to the south is the village of Kingston, with the tower of St James' Church visible on the skyline. To the north, the heathlands of Purbeck stretch out towards Poole Harbour and its islands.

5. With the castle to your back, follow the fence westward along the grassy top of the ridge. You'll pass a kissing gate before you reach an Ordnance Survey triangulation pillar.

6. Cross into the next field and continue westwards with the fence to your right.

7. Follow the fence until woodland rises up on your right. Then begin heading diagonally left towards the centre of the hedgerow, where you'll find a gate into the next field.

8. Continue along the ridgeway, past the Mary Baxter MBE commemoration stone and follow the path along the ridge until it descends to meet the road.

9. Cross the road and follow the green sign-post towards Steeple. A short, bramble-beset path will quickly lead to a stile. Climb over and take the path that gradually descends to the left.

10. When it is joined by a fence on the left, keep following the grassy track as it undulates for about a third of a mile, before meeting a gate.

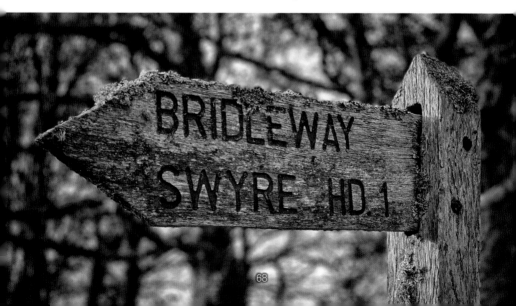

11. Follow the track downhill, ignoring the first gate on the left and the stiles. Also ignore a gate on the left leading to a field with a large barn. Instead, take the public footpath ahead and slightly to the right.

12. When you reach a gate on the left (opposite a large white stone embedded in the grass) go through it and follow the hedgerow down to a stile.

13. Take the farm track down to the road.

14. Turn left onto the road and, almost immediately, right onto another public footpath.

15. Follow the path as it snakes between the hedgerows and climb over a stile to emerge onto a large field

16. NB: **Here the path can be very indistinct depending on what has been planted in the fields, but even when the field is fallow, you can usually spot a lightly trodden path if you look carefully.** Follow the path diagonally right and south-west, through the middle of the field and continue roughly the same trajectory through the next field towards a stile on the opposite side.

17. Climb the double stile into a third field and continue in the same direction.

18. The exit to this field isn't entirely clear, but there is a gap in the field boundary right in the southern corner that leads you to a stile.

19. Cross the bridge, and snake to the right and through the trees, climbing another stile into a wide, open field. Continue uphill to the far right-hand (south-western) corner of the field where there is yet another stile.

20. After climbing over, head up a slightly steeper hill to the next stile which takes you out on to the road with views of Kimmeridge Bay and Clavell Tower ahead.

INFO: CLAVELL TOWER

This 35 foot tower was built in 1830 by Reverend John Richards Clavell as an observatory and folly. It's provided inspiration for the likes of Thomas Hardy and P.D. James and is now owned by the Landmark Trust. In an extraordinary move to save the tower from its precarious position atop Hen Cliff, the Landmark Trust disassembled the entire structure in 2006, relocating every one of the 16,272 stones and rebuilding the tower 80 feet inland. It is now one of the Trust's holiday lets and can accommodate two people with a 360 degree panorama of the surrounding coast and countryside. You don't get many hotel rooms with that kind of view!

Clavell Tower

21. Turn left onto the road, then in a few hundred yards, left again, followed by the first right, which leads south-eastwards up a rocky track until you meet a gate at the top.

THE VIEW: From this vantage point you can see the entire route walked so far, from Corfe Castle to the north-east, along the ridge of West Hill and Knowle Hill. The views to the south are no less impressive, with the strange angular shape of Gad Cliff rising up to the west, the white cliffs of Mupe Bay just protruding above it (all enjoyed in Walk 8).

22. Follow the path to the top of the hill and then continue as it curves south-east towards Swyre Head. In about a mile, you'll reach the final gate before the mound of the Swyre Head viewpoint.

THE VIEW: From the elevated position of Swyre Head's viewpoint, you can see not only back down the coast towards Kimmeridge in the west, but now also towards St Aldhelm's Head and its chapel to the east (enjoyed in Walk 5).

23. Once you've enjoyed the view, turn back and take the path north-east, following the drystone wall; Polar Wood will gradually rise to block the view on the left.

INFO: THE ENCOMBE ESTATE

Encombe Estate To your right, you'll notice the large country estate of Encombe. The estate was originally granted to the Abbess of Shaftesbury by King Eadred in A.D. 948 and remained in the possession of Shaftesbury Abbey until 1539, during the period of the dissolution of the monasteries. Quickly passing through two other owners, it was eventually acquired by the Culliford family in 1552 who kept it until 1734. Interestingly, the estate might well have been acquired by Oliver Cromwell had the Culliford family not provided men to help with the destruction of Corfe Castle in 1645. The property and estate are still privately owned. Amazingly, it has been owned by only six families in its 1,100 year history.

24. Continue through a large metal gate and into the next field, following the path as it curves to the left and eventually meets the road leading down into the Encombe Estate.

25. Cross the road and go through the gate into the car park, then turn right onto the road, which in about a mile, leads all the way to Kingston.

Corfe Castle

DETOUR: KINGSTON VILLAGE

Kingston boasts the beautiful church of St James - it's a stunning building and is usually open, so do take the opportunity to pop your head in if you have time. It was the venue for a Ninebarrow concert on Hallowe'en 2015! It's also well worth mentioning that while the walk continues back towards Corfe now, if you fancy a pint or some food, the Scott Arms is fantastic on both counts, with brilliant views from the garden down towards the Castle. You can reach it by continuing past the church.

26. Just before the first house as you enter the village, double back on yourself by taking a track on your left, then after a few yards, take the public footpath on the right.

27. Snake down the hill through woodland and then turn right onto a straight track. Just before the next 'Private' sign, take the gate and stile to the left, making a beeline for the castle as you continue to head downhill.

28. Take the stile through the hedge at the bottom of the field and then climb another stile, following the path along the right-hand edge of the field until you meet a farm track.

29. Cross the track and climb the stile, joining the Hardy Way, following the right-hand edge of the next field to the gate, and over the bridge. The path becomes a little tight here and involves a wee bit of stooping as you cross some boardwalks and eventually meet a gate.

30. Crossing out into the open, follow the path northwards, crossing two more bridges, before emerging onto Corfe Common.

31. Follow the path northwards and the castle will appear once again. There are a number of tracks criss-crossing Corfe Common, but keep heading generally towards the castle, aiming for a gate visible just to the right of the white house below the ruins.

32. When you meet the single-track road, turn right, crossing a cattle grid. Follow signs to Corfe, taking the road back into town.

33. When you reach The Square, continue almost to the Castle entrance but instead turn left past the Corfe Castle Tea Rooms and follow the path around the south-west side of the ruins. We love this end to the walk - giant, precarious chunks of masonry everywhere, and views of the castle from a very different angle to any the walk has offered so far. Follow the path down to the road.

34. Cross over the road, taking the wooden bridge, and turn right, following the Corfe River until you re-join the path from the start of the walk. This will lead you back to the car park. ●

Acknowledgements

We've had so much fun putting this book together and we're incredibly grateful to all the friends and family who have helped us out with so many aspects of this project. We couldn't have done it without you guys!

First and foremost, we want to thank Jon's mum, Julie Whitley, who has spent an inordinate amount of time helping us to proof-read the book. Her help and support has been absolutely invaluable.

Secondly, huge thanks to our hardy team of friends and family who have been such wonderful 'proof-walkers' (i.e. guinea pigs!):

Martin Byrne

Tim Davis

Sarah Dixon

Mark Edwards

Vicki LaBouchardiere

Fiona Revill

Rebecca Rosier

Tibor Stephenson Jung

Kevin Whitehouse

Bob Whitley

Julie Whitley

Freddie Williams

Kim Williams

Neil Williams

We're hugely indebted to Greg Funnell and his wife Steph for their time and creativity on the photo shoot which produced the fabulous cover photographs.

We'd also like to thank John and Kate Sibley for the amazing helicopter ride which enabled us to take the aerial photo for the Ninebarrow Walking Holidays advert towards the front of the book.

And last, but by no means least, we'd like to thank Jane Brace for all of her efforts on the publicity for this project.